BOOKSTORE

Tameside Public Libraries

No **181915** I   Class **780.924**
TAC

Date of Return $Doe, P.M.$

Oxford Studies of Composers

Oxford Studies of Composers (4)

TALLIS

PAUL DOE

London

OXFORD UNIVERSITY PRESS

NEW YORK   TORONTO

1976

Oxford University Press, Ely House, London W. 1

GLASGOW NEW YORK TORONTO MELBOURNE WELLINGTON
CAPE TOWN IBADAN NAIROBI DAR ES SALAAM LUSAKA ADDIS ABABA
DELHI BOMBAY CALCUTTA MADRAS KARACHI LAHORE DACCA
KUALA LUMPUR SINGAPORE HONG KONG TOKYO

ISBN 0 19 314122 1

First Published 1968
Second edition 1976

Printed in Great Britain
Photo-litho reprint by W & J Mackay Ltd, Chatham
from earlier edition

CONTENTS

INTRODUCTION

TALLIS'S composing career occupied roughly the central fifty years of the sixteenth century, spanning all the religious upheavals of that period, and coinciding with rapid and fundamental changes in the status and style of English church music. When he was pensioned off at the dissolution of Waltham Abbey in 1540, he had already served for at least ten years in varied monastic employment, quite unaffected by reforming activity. At some time late in Henry VIII's reign he was appointed a Gentleman of the Chapel Royal, a body of musicians engaged to sing and compose for the monarch's private services, where he became more directly exposed to the lucid and expressive techniques of continental musicians, as well as to the very different musical ideals of the puritans. He remained there until his death in 1585, composing for the official English liturgy under Edward VI (1547–53), and for the Latin rite again during its restoration under Mary Tudor (1553–8). Mary evidently regarded him as her principal composer, from whom music for an important occasion would be automatically commissioned. Elizabeth, officially Protestant, seems to have asked for both Latin and English church music, though in relatively small quantities and perhaps more for occasional than for normal liturgical use. Early in her reign a sharp decline in the standard of church music in general caused the Chapel Royal to act increasingly as a magnet for the best musicians, so that Tallis—by then its doyen—held a musical position of the greatest eminence in the land.

Until the Reformation, almost all musicians were employed as 'clerks', that is, as singing-men in a religious establishment. The post of organist was uncommon, the duties of playing the instrument (where one was used) being shared by the singing-men. A clerk who was also a composer thought of himself primarily as a craftsman in the service of the church, producing whatever was required of him: the parish-clerks of London even had their own guild, the Fraternity of St. Nicholas. Contemporary chroniclers and diarists like Machyn occasionally refer to a ceremonial Mass, but to them the composer is always as anonymous as the man who carved the choir-stalls.

Such an attitude explains why it was quite possible for a man like Tallis, if he avoided controversy, to continue to serve quietly under

7

any religious or political conditions; and also why it is essential that any account of his church music should stress its functional nature. In a sense, his surviving music is a mirror of its age. There is at least one example of almost every musical genre known to the English church in the sixteenth century (the chief exceptions being processional items and verse-music); and it reflects with astonishing clarity the bewildering changes of language and liturgy, the cross-currents of musical style and technique, and the advent of a humanist aesthetic of subjective interpretation of liturgical texts. It is hard to think of any other composer before 1600 who travelled such a distance stylistically, and almost incredible that such utterly different works as *Ave rosa sine spinis*, the seven-part Mass, the forty-part motet *Spem in alium* and the *Lamentations* (to mention only Latin compositions) could all have been written by the same person. Such diversity might suggest a merely routine composer, a dutiful craftsman and no more; yet Tallis at his best achieves that blend of technical mastery and personal expression which one associates with only a dozen or so of the greatest sixteenth-century masters.

Tallis's Latin church music, which must predominate in any balanced discussion of his work, is collected in *Tudor Church Music*, Vol. VI. The editors unfortunately failed to supply the plainsong needed to make the ritual items liturgically and musically complete; and two or three pieces which they perforce printed in a fragmentary state have since been taken nearer to restoration by the discovery of new sources. But despite these and many minor defects the volume is a serviceable basis for study, and figures in parentheses in my text refer to pages in that edition. Until recently the English church music had received no such systematic attention, but I have been both fortunate and privileged to be able to see, in advance of publication, part of a new complete edition prepared by Leonard Ellinwood for the series *Early English Church Music*, and I should like to thank both him and the general editor, Frank Ll. Harrison, for so kindly making this possible, and the British Academy for allowing me to quote from it my Exx. 33–36 inclusive. I should also like to record my gratitude to Mr. Jeremy Noble for the loan of his partial transcription of the seven-part Mass and for much other helpful information and discussion; for their help in various ways to my colleagues Professor Anthony Lewis, Dr. Nigel Fortune, Mr. David Greer and Mrs. Margaret Downes; and to Professor Joseph Kerman for reading the proofs and making a number of useful comments.

In a book of this kind it is not possible to avoid some relatively unfamiliar musical and liturgical terms. Most are explained, but for others the reader is recommended to consult Apel's *Harvard Dictionary of Music*. I have tried to include enough musical examples to give the reader without access to Tallis editions a clear idea of the composer's range of style and technique. For this reason, some of them tend to be 'convincing' rather than 'average' samples. For the sake of consistency I have, throughout, designated voices by the names current early in Tallis's lifetime, viz. Treble, Mean (=alto), Counter-tenor, Tenor, and Bass. The reduction of note-values is not consistent, since I prefer to conform with the principles adopted in most modern editions of Tudor church music: that is, the values are quartered for the early melismatic style, but halved for the later more syllabic or imitative styles. (In the eight examples where they are quartered, this is indicated.) The problems of tempo are unfortunately too complex for discussion in this small volume. The reader should also bear in mind that no single composition by Tallis can be dated with absolute certainty: my apparent preoccupation with this problem is attributable solely to my conviction that a chronology is a prerequisite of any worthwhile stylistic discussion.

I

THE OLD TRADITION

To judge from their surviving music, composers of the first forty years or so of the Tudor era (1485–1525) were concerned almost entirely with writing on a large scale in three liturgical forms: the Ordinary of the Mass, the votive antiphon, and the Magnificat. The second quarter of the sixteenth century, however, began to produce smaller and more modest versions of each of these forms for use on non-festal occasions (or in institutions with more limited choral resources), and also a significant number of polyphonic settings of other ritual items, such as the respond and hymn. Each of the earlier large forms remained an identifiable genre, but of steadily decreasing prominence, so that only a handful can be dated after 1540. Indeed Tallis himself contributed what may have been the last examples of the large votive antiphon and Mass.

We have some or all of five antiphons by Tallis, four large and one small. Though accurate dating is impossible, the first two listed here may well contain his earliest known music.

TCM (page)

169	*Ave rosa sine spinis*
144	*Salve intemerata virgo*
162	*Ave Dei patris*
123	*Gaude gloriosa*
98	*Sancte Deus* (small)

Whereas the cyclic Mass and Magnificat were both strictly liturgical forms, always set to the same text and sung in their proper ritual context, the votive antiphon was an independent composition usually performed as a separate devotional observance.[1] It was widely cultivated in collegiate foundations like Eton College and King's, Cambridge, in many of which the choir was bound by statute to process each evening to the chapel to sing an antiphon of the Virgin. A variety of texts was used for this purpose. Some were traditional and fairly short prose texts, like the four still used (one in each season of the church's year) at the end of Compline in the Roman rite; others, of more recent origin, were long and highly-mannered effusions, usually full of superlatives

---

[1] It had some affinity, in fact, with the later anthem, to which (by a curious freak of etymology) the name became transferred.

and often in rhyming stanzas. Thus *Salve intemerata* and *Gaude gloriosa* have prose texts,[2] the first rather rambling, the second more cogent with nine invocations each beginning 'Gaude'. *Ave rosa* and *Ave Dei patris*, on the other hand, each have a verse text of seven stanzas—a number widely associated with the Virgin, typically in the Feasts of the Seven Joys and Seven Sorrows. *Ave rosa* is actually a 'farsed' version of the *Ave Maria*, each of its first six verses beginning with a word or phrase of that text. *Ave Dei patris*, alone of these large antiphons, was widely set by other composers.[3]

In each case Tallis's musical design conforms closely to a long tradition which can still be observed in settings as late as Mary's reign. One of the principal features of large-scale composition early in the century was the clear division and sharp contrast between sections of the music set for sonorous full chorus, usually in five or more parts, and those for a small group of two or three (sometimes four) solo voices. The variety of groupings of solo voices could be increased by the device of 'gimel', meaning two voices from the same section of the choir. In *Gaude gloriosa*, for example, Tallis uses a quite exotic double gimel for four treble voices (131), later joined by a bass. However, such 'hollow' scoring was not unusual. A typical polyphonic antiphon was in two halves, the first in triple time and the second duple, each consisting of two solo sections (for different groups) followed by one full section. Naturally this design was capable of a good deal of adaptation and extension, but all four of Tallis's conform to it in broad outline. The shapeless text of *Salve intemerata* evidently gave him trouble: for instance, the prolonged density of the long final tutti is relieved by two very brief solo passages (157), probably inserted as an afterthought.

In point of style, Tallis's immediate musical heritage had its roots firmly in medieval tradition, and was only very sporadically beginning to show evidence of Renaissance ideals. Composers using the florid style in the early years of the century sought the maximum independence of voices, allowing each one quietly to pursue its own constantly changing melodic shapes, its own highly subtle rhythmic patterns set against other parts and against the prevailing pulse, yet always in conformity with a simple harmonic structure of $\frac{5}{3}$ and $\frac{6}{3}$ triads. In the full sections the effect is one of unceasing rhythmic vitality superimposed on a rich chordal sonority.

The extract from the early *Ave rosa*[4] in Ex. 1 illustrates this 'differ-

[2] Printed separately in *TCM*, pp. xxxiv–vi.
[3] Including Fayrfax, Taverner, Marbeck, and Robert Johnson.
[4] Material missing in *TCM* will all be found in *TCM Appendix*, p. 49, except for the section 'Benedicta tu' (174).

entiated' technique. Antiphons written after 1500 are rarely based on a cantus firmus,[5] but the tenor still has the appearance of being written first, followed by the bass and treble. These three voices determine the harmonic structure, and move more smoothly and logically than the mean and counter-tenor, which are often quite angular and awkward. Nevertheless, there is more freedom of part-movement here than is normal in Fayrfax and his generation (Ex. 1).

The solo sections are sometimes very florid indeed, to the point of

Ex. 1
(note-values 1/4)

TCM 171-2, App. 49

[5] A notable exception is Taverner's *Ave Dei Patris*, *TCM*, iii, p. 61.

requiring a virtuoso standard of singing. They do make a little more attempt to project the words by toying with syllabic imitative entries; on the other hand the melismas are even more protracted, those on the penultimate syllable sometimes extending to a third of the length of a verse:

Ex. 2
(note-values 1/4)

New stylistic features slowly emerging in the first half of the century can be classified under five main headings: repetition of musical 'sentences' and the idea of symmetry; the linear development of individual voices by scalewise movement, sequence, or systematic rhythmic organization; the integration of the texture by imitation; the introduction of harmonic tension by means of suspensions; and finally a decrease in melismatic writing and greater use of syllabic setting in both imitative and chordal textures.

As might be expected, individual composers were drawn to different aspects of this development. For example, Fayrfax, writing between 1490 and 1520, was already markedly less florid than most of his generation, and showed a distinct awareness of the concept of symmetry.[6] Taverner, on the other hand, although a decade or two later,

[6] A good example is the first verse of his Magnificat *O bone Iesu* (*EECM*, iv, p. 35), which is constructed in six well-defined phrases of 4–5 bars each, ending with a beautifully rounded Flemish cadence. It was undoubtedly this feeling for balance that caused him to be singled out by later historians.

was as florid and expansive as any of his predecessors. But in addition he was capable of cogent musical integration by the use of repeated rhythmic and melodic ideas, either imitatively or as ostinati within a single voice. Examples of this sort of writing can be found in Tallis's two early antiphons, most obviously in the vigorous play of imitative entries which traditionally builds the climax of the final 'Amen'. Elsewhere, however, he seems more concerned to avoid any purely musical tension. The enormous phrase-spans, instead of driving purposefully through to the cadence as Taverner liked them to do, usually relax before they reach it. This is not a fault, for Tallis is deliberately creating a static, contemplative structure. The large antiphon was a supremely impersonal musical speech, as spacious and remote as the lofty vaulted chapels that gave it birth.

Nevertheless, each has a distinct musical character. In *Salve intemerata* the texture is seldom imitative, but makes much use of melodic formulae reminiscent of third and fourth mode plainsongs such as those of the Purification. The tenor has some features of a cantus firmus (notably the cadence formula at the end of each half) but I have not been able to identify any plainsong in it. The formal problem created by the text is partly solved by a head-motive[7] technique, not common in antiphons. A harmonic problem, too, is the absence of a 'dominant' triad in the phrygian mode, compelling frequent plagal cadences which can sound repetitive (e.g. 145).[8] In his later phrygian-mode pieces, such as the first *Lamentations*, Tallis avoids this limitation by introducing B flats and moving freely outside the mode.

Ave Dei patris, which survives in a seriously incomplete state, is in duple time throughout, a feature that became increasingly common (and eventually standard) from about 1540 onwards.[9] However, the tender, meditative styles of this period can often be sung equally well in either measure. *Sancte Deus* illustrates the far more succinct small antiphon, marvellously effective with its ringing invocations. This widely-used Jesus text is symptomatic of the trend, under reformatory pressures, away from devotions of the Virgin.[10]

[7] A similar opening phrase for each main section.

[8] They are, however, much better without the indiscriminate G sharps which the editors of *TCM* have taken from Elizabethan MSS.

[9] There are a few wholly duple antiphons in the Peterhouse partbooks, e.g. Whytbrook's *Sancte Deus*.

[10] As an interesting instance, until 1540 the choristers of Salisbury daily sang a Mary-antiphon in memory of Bishop John Waltham; thereafter his bequest, which had been administered by the monastery of Edington, appears as a payment from the King 'for singing of an antiphon *Sancte Deus* before the Great Cross in the Nave of the Cathedral'. See *MMB*, p. 84.

Probably the latest, and certainly the finest, of these early pieces is the huge six-part *Gaude gloriosa*, which marks the culmination of the tradition of large antiphons. It is just possible that it dates from as late as Mary's reign, when the form was briefly revived.[11] There is still the sharp contrast of solo and full sections, still an unrelieved density in the latter. But the parts are here completely equated, with no question of a pre-existent tenor, and massive sets of imitative entries are woven into the six-part writing (though they are not used to shape the music in any way):

Ex. 3
(note-values 1/4)

TCM 139-40

[11] In *EECM*, ii, Harrison has published two large six-part antiphons by William Mundy, who in 1542-3 was still a choirboy at Westminster Abbey.

The long arching phrases show Tallis now taking more interest in Taverner's methods of melodic and rhythmic organization than hitherto (e.g. the second section, 124–6); and some musical imagery is also in evidence, such as the long downward scale on 'portasti', and the sudden entry of the full chorus for 'omnia serviunt' (126). In its design and part-writing this is a masterly display of technical skill, albeit in an archaic mould. It is a work of truly medieval grandeur, which, if written for Mary, would have perfectly symbolized the old order which she so staunchly championed.

Tallis's three Masses represent three totally different methods of treating the form. The earliest is undoubtedly the 'derived' Mass[12] *Salve intemerata virgo* (3), whose parent-antiphon has already been discussed.[13]

The technique of creating a cyclic Mass by using some or all of the fabric of an existing composition had appeared on the continent before 1500, and was used on occasion by both Fayrfax and Taverner.[14] Normally no more than the beginning and end of each movement correspond with those of the antiphon, but Tallis's twin works are much more closely related, only about a quarter of the Mass being newly composed. Each movement begins with bars 1–3 and 13–15 of the antiphon (144), adapting this material as the text demands. The whole of the remainder of the Gloria, except for two very brief passages, is based on six other sections of the antiphon. The Credo uses the opening and three further long sections of the antiphon, but here there are two large new insertions: from 'Crucifixus' to 'secundum scripturas' (15–17) and from 'et exspecto' to the end. The Sanctus is similar, with two new passages (including the Benedictus) while the Agnus has one (Qui tollis). Apart from the common opening, Tallis has not used any section of the antiphon twice, but all of it is transplanted except for the passage from 'Tu nimirum' (149) to the double bar.

Owing to the melismatic style Tallis had little difficulty in adapting the material to new text. The few true emendations which do occur throw an interesting light on the composer's evolution towards a more purposeful melodic style. Ex. 4 shows one:

---

[12] Or 'parody' Mass, a term which (as Lewis Lockwood has recently shown) had no currency in the sixteenth century. See L. Lockwood, 'On "parody" as term and concept in 16th-century music', *Aspects of Medieval and Renaissance Music: a Birthday Offering to Gustave Reese* (London, 1967), p. 560.

[13] Both are found in the Peterhouse part-books (*c.* 1540). The antiphon is also in MS. Harley 1709, f. 46v, which could well be appreciably earlier.

[14] E.g. his *Mater Christi, TCM*, iii, p. 92 (antiphon) and i, p. 99 (Mass).

More remarkable, perhaps, is the stylistic disparity between the antiphon material and the five substantial new sections. Some are almost incongruous—particularly the end of the Credo and the long new passage in the Agnus (28), with its splendid bass ostinato. Nevertheless, the joinery is highly ingenious, and the total effect more compelling than that of the antiphon. It is a work of festal proportions, perfectly adequate for its purpose, but not in any sense great music.[15]

The extant short Masses of this period are distinguished from the large forms not only in size, but also in that none has a title connecting it with a major feast. Many are within the compass of men's voices and may simply be for non-festal Sunday Mass, or possibly even for ferial use, in connexion with the increasing daily observance of Lady-Mass. They exhibit a remarkable diversity of style and method, ranging from the extended and elaborate treatment of Taverner's *Western Wynde*[16] to the deliberately simple and seemingly experimental sort of texture found in his *Playn Song* Mass,[17] in which he uses only three note-

[15] Mss. Add. 18936–9 contain the first section of *Gaude gloriosa*, but without text and headed 'Qui tollis' (62). H. B. Collins, in *Music and Letters*, x (1929), p. 157, suggested that this might be a remnant of another parody Mass. However it is more likely that it was simply extracted for instrumental use and mistitled. *Domine Deus* (62) and *Rex sanctorum* (298), from the same source, are almost certainly similar fragments of lost compositions—if indeed they are by Tallis at all.

[16] *TCM*, i, p. 3.

[17] ibid., p. 30.

values—the breve, semibreve and (after a dotted semibreve only) the minim.[18] The unnamed four-part Mass by Tallis (31) is very much in this latter category. It uses a wider range of note-values than Taverner's *Playn Song*, but is even more consistently syllabic—an almost perfect embodiment of Cranmer's express wish for music 'not full of notes, but, as near as may be, for every syllable a note, so that it may be sung distinctly and devoutly':[19]

Ex. 5

TCM 31

This extract burgeons into the most modest melisma at the cadence; in only three or four passages can any protracted melisma be found:

[18] The same values, in fact, that Marbeck uses in his *Book of Common Prayer Noted* of 1550, where they are called 'strene', 'square' and 'pycke' notes. This rhythmic structure, rather than the melodic style, is probably the explanation for the title of the Mass, for it is known from contemporary faburdens that certain types of plainsong—among them Lady-Mass Kyries, the psalm-tones, and certain processional pieces—were performed in simple measured polyphony using only these note-values. Marbeck's adoption of the same sort of rhythmic structure may indicate that it had been quite widely applied to plainsong. Indeed the enigmatic Mass-title 'Upon the square' probably implies no more than a cantus firmus of this type.

[19] Letter to the King, 1544, referring to vernacular processional music. This Mass was almost certainly written at about the same time.

Several other important stylistic features of this Mass also reflect new trends. No longer are there 'block' contrasts of texture: four parts are used throughout, with only brief reductions to two or three voices (as at 'Domine fili', 32). Further, Tallis does not set the text straight through in each voice. There is some carefully calculated repetition of phrases—seven in the Gloria, for instance. Always the repeat is slightly varied: it may be more extended, or in sequence at a higher pitch, or simply more fully scored.

The Mass has much affinity with Tallis's early English anthems, though it is doubtful whether the style stands up to such extended use. The music is carefully shaped (notice the octave fall, and gradual rise again, of the top part of Ex. 5); there are periodic contrasts of texture; and the music is harmonically well controlled, with ingeniously varied cadences. But the combined effect of melodic, harmonic, and rhythmic restraint is inevitably one of dullness. There is no real harmonic tension: dissonant suspensions are rare except at cadences, where today they sound merely conventional. Above all, perhaps, the relative dearth of imitation is an effective demonstration of its value as a form-building procedure.

If the two Masses so far discussed are not intrinsically great works, the seven-part *Puer natus est nobis* is of quite different stature. The editors of *TCM* were able to print only fragments of it (49–61), but we now have the whole of the Gloria and virtually all the Sanctus.[20] It is

---

[20] Discovered, in partbooks belonging to the Madrigal Society, by Joseph Kerman, who also identified the cantus firmus. The two movements here discussed have been transcribed by Jeremy Noble.

revealed as a cantus firmus Mass on a very large festal scale, of a kind much used early in the century, but of which no example from later than about 1540 was hitherto known.[21] Stylistic features of this work, however, point strongly to the reign of Mary, and the cantus firmus (the Introit *Puer natus est nobis*) identifies it as a Christmas Mass. As Jeremy Noble has suggested, the most likely occasion for its performance was Christmas 1554, when Philip of Spain was still in London after his marriage to Mary. Less than a month earlier (30 November) Cardinal Pole had pronounced his formal absolution of the nation. On the first Sunday in Advent (2 December) Mass was celebrated with great splendour in St. Paul's Cathedral[22]—and almost certainly (although we have no record) again on Christmas Day. It is even possible that the choice of the Introit, 'Puer natus est nobis et filius datus est nobis cuius imperium super humerum eius . . .', may not have been wholly unconnected with the then highly topical news that Mary was expecting an heir.

Earlier treatment of the cantus firmus in large English Masses had varied a good deal. A typical layout, like that of Fayrfax's *Regali ex progenie*, might have two statements in each movement, the first triple and the second duple. Taverner's *Gloria tibi trinitas*[23] has a third statement, in diminution, in each; but on the whole proportional treatment and other artifice are rare. Tallis sets both Gloria and Sanctus in duple time throughout.[24] The cantus firmus, consisting of the first four phrases of the plainsong, is stated once in the Gloria in long note-values. The Sanctus, however, is more subtle: it begins with the first phrase in strict diminution, then immediately repeats it in an exact retrograde version. The remainder now proceeds normally, except that various neumes of the plainsong are stated twice—in two cases backwards. The long notes of the chant are much split up to accommodate the Mass-text, but by comparing different statements of it one can deduce that its basic rhythmic layout[25] is as in Ex. 7, suggesting that Tallis set it approximately as it might have been chanted—though of course in very slow motion. If this is so it provides useful evidence of the rhythmic treatment of plainsong at this date.

---

[21] Marbeck's *Per arma iustitiae* was perhaps the latest (*TCM*, x, p. 165).

[22] *The Diary of Henry Machyn, 1550–63*, ed. J. G. Nichols (Camden Society, London, 1848), p. 77. ('Both the queen's chapel and the king's and Paul's choir sang.') There is no entry for Christmas Day.

[23] *TCM*, i, p. 126.

[24] The Benedictus is however in 'tempus perfectum' in Tenbury MSS. 341–4.

[25] The units are semibreves in the Gloria, minims in the Sanctus. It is clear that Tallis always sets neumes in equal values. The rests vary in length.

Ex. 7
(first phrase only)

As in the four-part Mass, there are no block divisions of full and reduced textures, a very high proportion being full. Even the Benedictus is reduced for no more than the first few bars. But passages of lighter scoring are skilfully interwoven, often associated with repetition of text, and most frequently occurring during rests in the cantus firmus. Both movements begin with a block-chord head-motive; and the second major section in each ('Qui tollis' and 'Pleni' respectively) begins with sustained fugal imitation in the current continental vein—without perhaps quite the feeling for 'line' that characterizes the work of Josquin's pupils at their best (Ex. 8).

Elsewhere Tallis does not attempt this sort of 'weighty' imitation, because the long notes of the tenor, sometimes lasting eight bars or more, compel a very slow rate of harmonic change. Nevertheless, he is

Ex. 8   TCM 49

just as resourceful as any foreign contemporary in devising imitative and other textures in this situation. The points, shaped melodically in repeated notes and thirds, are mostly brought in on three or four declamatory notes in an up-beat pattern. They enter singly, in pairs, in larger groups, once or twice even in block antiphony between groups of three voices:

TCM 53

A favourite method is the entry of a single part on an up-beat, followed on the next by three or four other voices simultaneously. Very little of the writing is florid in the old sense, although prominent melismas are periodically interwoven, beautifully exploiting the vocal colours and setting off the syllabic material:

Ex. 10

TCM 60-1

The combination of slow harmony and up-beat patterns gives this work, despite its sonority, a rhythmic buoyancy and momentum unprecedented in England. Indeed, there is unquestionably continental influence here—perhaps the most likely single source being Gombert, who was associated with the Imperial chapel in various capacities from 1526 onwards, and who was almost certainly in Madrid for some time between then and 1554. His music, published by Attaingnant from 1541 onwards, includes a six-part Mass *Quam pulchra es*,[26] with a seven-part

[26] *Opera Omnia (Corpus Mensurabilis Musicae)*, iii.

Agnus on a cantus firmus. The brief extract from this movement in Ex. 11 should be compared with Ex. 10: it illustrates some affinity in the layout of the texture and the shaping of a phrase—as well as Tallis's much slower cantus firmus and lingering medieval expansiveness.

Ex. 11

Gombert, *Opera omnia* iii

If Tallis was indeed writing for the combined English and Spanish chapels he must have felt very much 'on trial'. The challenge was superbly met, however, for this 'international' work forms as impressive a climax to a half-century of English festal Masses as does the very insular *Gaude gloriosa* to the tradition of large antiphons. It is certainly one of the finest products of the generation between Taverner and Byrd.[27]

27 Further on Tallis's early church music, see my paper 'Latin Polyphony under Henry VIII', *Proceedings of the Royal Musical Association*, xcv (1968–9), p. 81.

II

RITUAL MUSIC OF THE MID-CENTURY

I T is convenient to group into this next chapter all that music (written chiefly for the office or Lady-Mass) in which only part of the plainsong is replaced by polyphony, and which does not make musical or liturgical sense unless the remaining plainsong is interpolated. The main forms concerned are the hymns and Magnificat, in which alternate verses were set, and the office responds, which until the Reformation were almost universally sung between the chapter and the hymn, but which are now largely confined to monastic rites.

The Magnificat, alone of these three, had a fairly long history of polyphonic composition in England, having earlier attracted some very elaborate treatment, in common with the Mass and votive antiphon. We have no such large-scale Magnificat by Tallis, his one surviving pre-Reformation setting being in four parts and of relatively small dimensions (64). Nevertheless, it can only be understood in the light of a rather extraordinary technique of composition whose mysteries have not yet been fully penetrated.

In its simple plainsong form the Magnificat was sung antiphonally to one of the normal eight psalm-tones, the twelve verses (counting the doxology) being intoned by each half of the choir alternately. From as early as the fourteenth century the practice had developed of adorning the six even-numbered verses with a simple form of improvised polyphony by adding a part below the plainsong, sometimes mainly in thirds but occasionally with more freedom, as in this example of the first Tone:[1]

Ex. 12(a) Sarum plainsong

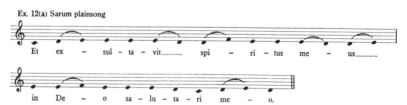

[1] From a fifteenth-century source, MS. Lansdowne 462, f. 152. The chant (upper part) is not in the MS. but can be supplied without difficulty, at least in broad outline. The ornamental cadences were a standard feature.

This sort of treatment also existed in various three-part forms, one beginning as in Ex. 13:[2]

Ex. 13
(note-values 1/4)

It seems, however, that a three-part 'setting' of this kind most frequently consisted of parallel $^6_3$ chords, with an $^8_5$ on the first note and at the ends of phrases. This is the form (known as *faburden*) in which it was improvised, and of which we therefore have practically no record. The few examples surviving were written down only because the parts deviate sufficiently from a parallel path to make notation necessary or helpful. Certain deviations became traditional: in these first-Tone versions, in particular, the broad outline of the lowest part remained astonishingly consistent over very long periods.[3]

The full-choral Magnificat in late medieval England seems to have evolved directly from these humble prototypes. A further part was added at the bottom, the lowest part of the faburden becoming the

---

[2] MS. Add. 4911, f. 98, a treatise of the late sixteenth century. The author was describing a practice no longer current in his day, and seems mistaken in implying that the top part is the chant.

[3] See F. Ll. Harrison, 'Faburden in Practice', *Musica Disciplina*, xvi (1962), p. 11. It will be noticed that the two-part example quoted starts on a unison, whereas in the three-part version the lowest part starts a fifth below the plainsong and rises a fourth. Some other much-used chants, notably the hymn *Salve festa dies*, had similar alternative forms for the beginning.

tenor of the larger setting, while the chant itself was ornamented out of existence in the florid upper parts. As the form expanded, the tenor, too, became greatly elaborated, but in most settings, including that of Tallis (64) (Ex. 14)[4], its origin is unmistakable.

Magnificat composition on a faburden tenor persisted right up to the Reformation, only a few late settings adopting the continental

Ex. 14
(note-values 1/4; transposed down a fourth)

TCM 64

---

[4] The chant required for the odd-numbered verses is the first Tone, ending on G; or (at this transposed pitch) beginning on C and ending on D, exactly as in Ex. 12 above. An odd consequence of this arrangement is that the final of the polyphonic verses is a fifth below the final note of the plainsong; yet no other available ending is possible. A further unusual feature of this setting is that the cantus firmus is twice transferred to other voices in later verses.

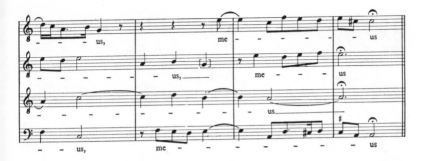

practice of using the psalm-Tone itself as a cantus firmus. The faburden origin, and the force of tradition, dictated the 'differentiated' and rhythmically wayward manner of the opening half-verse quoted. Later there is occasionally found some vigorous free imitation (e.g. 'implevit bonis', 69). The resulting mixture of styles is characteristic of Taverner's generation, but here does not achieve that composer's driving force.

Until about 1525 in England there are only sporadic instances of the use of polyphony in the daily office other than in the Magnificat, the chief item of the Ordinary. The following decades, however, saw an increasing participation of full choirs in the Proper of the office, mainly in the Vespers responds and hymns, but also in other offices, especially where some particular ceremony was involved. Tallis's contribution to this repertory is all associated with the Sarum rite, and therefore almost certainly composed before its final abandonment in 1559. Three small responds in the Gyffard partbooks may well be Henrician:

TCM		Office	AS plate
90	*Audivi vocem*	All Saints (Matins)	567
92	*Hodie nobis caelorum rex*	Christmas (Matins)	47
94	*In pace si dedero*	First Sunday in Lent until Passion Sunday (Compline)	150

Since the polyphonic setting of these smaller responds differs fundamentally from that of the large ones, it may be helpful to explain the liturgical form. Responsorial singing consists of one or more solo verses, each followed by a choral response[5] (a kind of refrain) which is also sung at the beginning. In Ex. 15:

[5] The term 'response' has no liturgical authority but is used here to distinguish the choral part from the 'respond' or 'responsory', meaning the complete form.

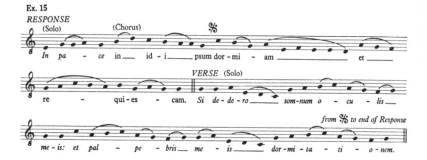

the first half is the response, all choral except for the incipit 'In pace', which is sung by a soloist in the usual manner. The solo verse 'Si dedero' is followed by a shortened repeat of the response, beginning at *al segno*. Many responds, including *Audivi* and *Hodie*,[6] consist of no more than this ABA structure, but *In pace* (unusually) has a second verse, the 'Gloria patri', sung to the same chant as 'Si dedero', and followed by the complete response again. A glance at the three Tallis settings will show that only the solo sections—the incipit and verse(s) of each—are set in polyphony, which does not make even grammatical sense without the choral plainsong.[7]

It may be that the lack of a decisive personality in his early years, combined with the stimulus of moving from monastic to more varied secular employment after 1540, enabled Tallis gradually to transform his style through the middle decades of the century, keeping fully abreast of current trends in technique and taste. In these small responds, perhaps for the first time, he uses imitation as the chief structural principle: the points are not superimposed on the texture in the 'ostinato' fashion of the early antiphons, but become instead the very stuff of the music, interweaving and overlapping cadences, and themselves dictating the shape of the phrases and the form of the whole. In the extract from *In pace* in Ex. 16 (the second half of the verse)

---

[6] The two Matins responds were ceremonial. The Sarum Customary prescribes that *Audivi* is to be sung by four or five boys, and polyphonic settings always provide a break in mid-verse (before 'Ecce sponsus', see 91) where they turned from the altar to the choir. *Hodie*, similarly, was to be sung by five boys 'in a raised place above the altar'. Tallis's settings both lie within a compass of two octaves, and therefore may well have been designed for boys' voices.

[7] In one modern edition of *Audivi* the whole text of the response has been fitted to Tallis's music for the incipit.

each point is closely based on the corresponding phrase of plainsong (Ex. 15), in the manner of the imitative paraphrase techniques developed on the continent a generation earlier by Josquin, Isaac, and their contemporaries. The rising four-note scale, which for 'somnum' Tallis leaves in minims,

Ex. 17

TCM 95

(M.) som - num o - cu - - - - - lis

is for 'dormitationem' pictorially decorated with a nodding dotted rhythm; indeed the music is deliberately protracted to suggest somnolence. But for all the seamless flow and balancing cadences, he does not achieve the superbly logical symmetry of Josquin and his pupils at their best. He has learnt all the grammatical conventions of the style, and is equally aware of its expressive capabilities; but not until his Elizabethan period does one feel that these two aspects are completely integrated, with an automatic instead of a calculated response to the text. *Hodie* is the shortest and perhaps the most stylish of these three: it is vigorous and almost wholly syllabic, with the wide melodic intervals that were to become a prominent feature of Tallis's late style, and with hardly a trace of plainsong present.

The six larger responds occupy a more significant place in Tallis's output.

TCM		*Voices*	*Feast*	*AS plate*
186	[*Candidi*] *facti sunt Nazarei*	5	Apostles	H8
257	[*Dum transisset*] *Sabbatum*	5	Easter	236
282	[*Homo*] *quidam fecit coenam*	6	Corpus	—
237	[*Honor*] *virtus et potestas*	5	Trinity	290
272	[*Loquebantur*] *variis linguis*	7	Whitsun	277
293	[*Videte*] *miraculum*	6	Purification	395

Here it is not the solo but the choral part of the respond which is set: each consists, in fact, of no more than the response itself, minus the incipit (in square brackets) which is left to the soloist. The solo verse is followed by a partial repeat of the polyphonic response, beginning at a point which in four of these settings the *TCM* editors have indicated by repeat signs.[9] A second major departure is the presence, in all of them, of the choral plainsong itself, sung as a cantus firmus in equal semibreves throughout.[10] Tallis places it in the tenor in all except *Dum transisset* (treble) and *Homo quidam* (counter-tenor, but possibly wrongly entered in the Christ Church partbooks). This 'reversed' procedure and monorhythmic plainsong are first found in Taverner's earlier settings of *Dum transisset*,[11] the type becoming a popular form for major feasts. The equal-note cantus firmus imposes a semibreve 'harmonic rhythm' on the music; that is, a regular rate of chord change against which the composer can use expressive suspensions (Ex. 18).

[8] Follows plate 608.

[9] In *Videte miraculum* it is at 'stans onorata' (295, bar 6). In *Honor virtus* the repeat of 'in perenni saeculorum tempore' is fully written out, but there should of course be a break for the verse in 240, bar 3.

[10] We have now observed the three rhythmic methods of presenting a plainsong cantus firmus in Tallis's lifetime: the 'free' rhythm, greatly augmented, in the Mass; the mannered rhythm of fifteenth-century popular polyphony, found in faburden-influenced pieces; and the equal-note layout of these responds.

[11] *TCM*, iii, pp. 37, 43.

This harmonically-controlled sort of texture, already a classic procedure on the continent, was just beginning to crystallize in England: the cantus firmus is probably a symptom of a new style, rather than a conditioning factor. Tallis uses it to produce an effect of great solemnity, with a pulsating harmonic richness. The full chorus is used almost continuously, but with some variation of texture or material to suit succeeding phrases of text. The rhythmic and melodic contrasts, although less strongly marked than in Byrd's few cantus firmus works a generation later, are quite enough to offset any effect of monotony. These are festal works, and there is no question of any subjective treatment. Nevertheless, there is some imaginative writing, such as the vigorous racing pseudo-canon (first declamatory, then in brilliant melismatic 'alleluyas') in *Candidi facti sunt* (187); the deliberately complex texture and garrulous voices of *Loquebantur variis linguis*, with its seven parts in a compass of twenty notes; the effect of hushed wonderment achieved at the beginning of *Videte miraculum;* and later in the same piece the incessant A minor cadences for 'stans onorata' (295). This last respond, for all its aloofness, is both technically and imaginatively one of Tallis's really great works.

The only other significant composer of large responds at this time was Sheppard.[12] He and Tallis were also apparently the only two composers to produce hymn-settings in any real number: there survive eight by Tallis, all in five parts, and about fifteen by Sheppard, for five to eight voices. Indeed their joint output of both hymns and responds suggests that they had in mind some sort of annual cycle of office poly-phony, which must surely have been for Mary Tudor's chapel. As in the Magnificat, only even-numbered verses of hymns were set poly-phonically, the remainder (including the first) being sung in plainsong. The following list of Tallis's hymns identifies the first line of each, which is not given in *TCM*. The last column indicates a modern printed source of each plainsong,[13] which Tallis always sets in the highest voice (although Sheppard, in three of his hymns, transfers it to other voices).

TCM	Hymn	Liturgical occasion	Plainsong
264	Deus tuorum militum	Common of one martyr	EH 181
285	Iam Christus astra ascenderat	Pentecost	LU 866
289	Iesu salvator saeculi	Sunday after Easter	AM 163
261	Quod chorus vatum	Purification	—
242	Salvator mundi Domine	Christmas Day to octave of Epiphany	AS 46[14]
193	Sermone blando angelus[15]	Low Sunday to Ascension	EH 124
214	Te lucis ante terminum	Compline	AS 6[16]
215	Te lucis ante terminum	Compline	AM 34

All except *Deus tuorum militum* have the first one or two verses in triple time,[17] thereafter changing to duple. Where this triple metre is operative the cantus firmus is usually fairly freely treated rhythmically (e.g. *Iesu Salvator*) but occasionally adopts a regular trochaic tread (e.g. *Quod chorus*). In *Iam Christus* it is organized so as to create a strict canon between treble and counter-tenor. In a duple rhythm, however,

[12] A selection of six of his responds (edited by F. Ll. Harrison) is published in *Das Chorwerk*, lxxxiv (Wolfenbüttel, 1960).

[13] In the *English Hymnal* (*EH*), *Hymns Ancient and Modern* (*AM*), *Liber Usualis* (*LU*), or *Antiphonale Sarisburiensis* (*AS*). All, including *Quod chorus vatum*, can be found in the printed Sarum hymnal of 1528.

[14] The same tune as that of *Veni creator spiritus* (*EH* 154). See *AM* (Historical edition), p. xxxvi.

[15] Part of the long hymn *Aurora lucis rutilat*. See *MR*, p. 604.

[16] The same tune as that of *Iesu salvator saeculi* (*AM* 163).

[17] The 'triple' time is in fact *tempus imperfectum prolatio maior*, or in modern terms a 6/8 rather than 3/4. Both this archaic rhythm and the habit of setting the chant in the treble are probably survivals of fifteenth-century practice. *Deus tuorum* may be by Sheppard.

the chant is set out in regular semibreves, much as in the responds: only in the last verse of *Salvator mundi Domine* is there any significant ornamentation (244; it is in fact a metrical doxology). The chant is always very clearly recognizable, for Tallis never uses the more subtle paraphrase technique later found in Byrd (for example in his *Pange lingua* setting[18]). The added parts are always splendidly rich: although usually loosely imitative, they enter in quick succession, and often in pairs, to build up immediate sonority:

Ex. 19: *Iam Christus*, doxology.

18 *TCM*, vii, p. 134.

Now and again the 'points' are quite closely derived from the plainsong, but normally they are either unrelated or echo just one melodic interval. However, one verse is constructed of a complete five-part imitation of the plainsong semibreves, for the words 'Ob hoc precatu supplici' (265). In two hymns, *Iam Christus* and *Sermone blando*, the same music is used for more than one verse. Since *Te lucis* has no more than three verses, Tallis sets only the second, 'Procul recedant somnia'. There are two settings (214 and 215), one for each of the two tunes then in normal use. The second is a striking instance of completely homophonic writing.

The hymn *O nata lux de lumine* (209) does not belong to this Marian set, but is almost certainly Elizabethan. It does not use the plainsong (*EH* 234), nor is it set *alternatim*: the polyphony comprises the first and second verses, with a most unliturgical repeat of the last two lines. This, too, is almost wholly homophonic, and organized into a suppliant ostinato rhythm.

There remain for discussion two small samples of music for the Lady-Mass, both probably fairly early. *Euge caeli porta*[19] (179) is a solitary verse from the sequence *Ave praeclara*, for which Tallis probably set all the even-numbered verses. The single *Alleluya* (88) is one of a collection, by various composers, in the Gyffard partbooks. It has a number of features untypical of Tallis, notably four very widely spaced voices with some long rests, producing a texture which is vigorous but relatively ethereal and unsonorous. It is performed in the same manner as the large responds: the incipit 'Alleluya' is solo, the polyphony being the remainder of the response, with the plainsong in the alto. The verse 'Ora pro nobis' is not set.

The two middle decades of the sixteenth century produced an unbelievable jumble of musical forms and styles. It included all the early English service music and anthems, as well as most of the Latin music discussed so far. This was a period of conflict and overlap, not only of Catholic and reformed churches, but also of medieval and Renaissance outlook in life, religion, and art. Gothic luxuriance and remoteness vied with Renaissance logic and symmetry, ritual splendour with Puritan simplicity. The Marian office music has a curious ambivalence in this respect, for it possesses a lucidity of form and phrase-structure altogether new in Latin church music, yet at the same time the starkly objective cantus firmus imposes a detached, cold quality on the music. It has the technical refinement but not the humanity of Renaissance art. Yet even the process of refinement was to continue for nearly half a century, reaching a stage of maximum 'purity' in Morley

[19] The *TCM* text is obviously defective.

and one or two of his disciples. For Mary's and most of Elizabeth's reigns there still lingered a characteristic English enthusiasm, a love of sonority, of colourful melodic line and rich dissonance (like that in Ex. 19)—in short, a conservative tradition, on to which continental ideas were progressively grafted.

III

THE ELIZABETHAN MOTETS

IF it was fortunate for the nation that Elizabeth did not share the fierce Spanish piety of her half-sister Mary, she had none the less inherited her father's love of ceremony. Her quarrels with the recusants mainly concerned their allegiance to the Pope, which she regarded as treasonable; but formal religious observance as such, with a Latin liturgy and ornaments, she valued as much as they did. She was prudent enough not to resist the re-establishment of the 1552 prayer-book, as part of the Settlement of 1559. Within a year, however, there was published Walter Haddon's Latin translation of the prayer-book (*Liber precum publicarum*) with the queen's express wish that it be used in the two universities and in the public schools. By this time the seats of learning were evidently too strongly Protestant to accept it, but there is little doubt that it found some use in her own chapel.

For a few years it seemed that polyphony in church worship might be prohibited altogether. The puritans who opposed the vestments also tried hard to banish 'all curious singing and playing of the organ'. But they were narrowly defeated, and the official position remained as formulated in a royal injunction of 1559:

For the comforting of such that delight in music, it may be permitted that, in the beginning, or in the end of the Common prayers, either at Morning or Evening, there may be sung an Hymn, or suchlike song to the praise of Almighty God in the best sort of melody and Music that may conveniently be devised, having respect that the sentence of Hymn may be understood and perceived.[1]

In practice, for a decade or two after 1559, there is no evidence of any extensive cultivation of church polyphony in the country as a whole, apart from various simple forms of psalm-singing. Nor have we any documentary record of music in the Queen's chapel. But the fact that

[1] *Injunctions given by the Queen's Majesty* (London, 1559), No. 49.

Latin polyphony was sung there can be inferred from her known views and the surprisingly vigorous production of it by its composing members, such as Byrd, Parsons, William Mundy, and the now elderly Tallis.

Two pieces by Tallis, the paired *Magnificat* and *Nunc dimittis* (73, 85), were fairly clearly written for evensong of the Latin prayer-book.[2] The bulk of the Latin texts of this period, however, come from a variety of other sources. Some are complete psalms, mostly (but not always) using the Vulgate version; some correspond with antiphon or respond texts of the Sarum or Roman rites; others are merely prayers or collects. But whereas the ritual pieces of Mary's reign usually have Sarum plainsongs, and were composed for an identifiable feast in a manner befitting the occasion, the Elizabethan works only very seldom use a plainsong of any kind, and frequently have other characteristics as well which tend to confirm that no such narrowly liturgical purpose was intended. The manner of composition may be inappropriate to the normal liturgical situation of the words,[3] or there may be some textual deviation; or again some feature of the musical setting may be incompatible with pre-1559 usage. For example, the text of *In manus tuas* (202) is a well-known Compline respond, but Tallis has set both the response and the verse complete, with no full-close at the end of the response. The last third of the setting is repeated after a complete break (in which the doxology may have been intoned); but this repeat includes the verse, and therefore conforms to no known ritual procedure.[4] Similarly *Salvator mundi salva nos* (two settings, 216 and 219) becomes probably a Holy Week motet, and the Magnificat-antiphon *O sacrum convivium* a Communion motet. *O salutaris hostia*, officially the fifth verse of a hymn (*Verbum supernum prodiens*), is likewise set independently and could perhaps have been admitted to Haddon's Latin Communion as a sacrament motet.[5] In sum, Tallis is simply drawing on texts with particular meanings or associations as and when occasion

---

[2] Polyphonic settings of the old Compline *Nunc dimittis* were unknown, except for the Purification, when the canticle was sung *in extenso* with its antiphon *Lumen* during the distribution of candles. MS. Add. 5665, f. 62v has one of *c*. 1500, based on a faburden of the eighth Tone. But a *Magnificat-Nunc dimittis* 'pair' for the old rite would have been inconceivable.

[3] An extreme case is *Spem in alium*, the text of which is a ferial Matins respond in most rites.

[4] There are 'respond-motets' of this kind by other composers, such as Parsons and Byrd. For a discussion of the form, see Oliver Strunk, 'Some Motet-Types of the 16th Century', *Papers Read at the International Congress of Musicology, New York, 1939* (New York, 1944), p. 155.

[5] A purpose for which the same text was used on the continent, e.g. Lassus, *Complete Works*, v, p. 79. In Pierre de la Rue's *Missa de Sancta Anna*, a setting of it replaces Osanna I (see *MR*, p. 270).

demands, to provide devotional or ceremonial music, which was probably used before or after services, but was in general quite independent of them. It is a repertory of motets whose function was similar to that of the earlier votive antiphons—not only in situation, but also in the outlet thereby provided for the exercise of a hard-learned craft and the continuance of a tradition. Whether or not it was used in the Queen's chapel or other places of worship, most of it found its way into the numerous later MS. anthologies clearly designed for domestic use.

The English composer's new freedom to choose his own text for this kind of motet composition was, of course, one that had long been enjoyed abroad. Indeed it was at least half a century after Josquin had set the two laments of David, *Planxit autem David* and *Absalom fili mi*, before music of a comparable expressive power appeared in England in the 1560s. Nor, even then, did Tallis feel able or inclined to turn to the tragic figures of the Bible, for his works in this vein use texts drawn from liturgical, not biblical, sources. They thus retain a sort of objectivity, as though to allow the composer to remain almost wholly the craftsman, in no way identified with the actual sufferer. Two of them, *Derelinquat impius* (189) and *In ieiunio et fletu* (198), occur as Roman responds for the first Sunday of Lent;[6] while the *Lamentations* are settings of some of the readings for the offices of Holy Week. Tallis's first set of *Lamentations* (102–9) consists of one such reading, viz. two biblical verses each prefaced by a Hebrew letter ('Aleph' and 'Beth'). The second (110–22), which is a separate reading and therefore musically a quite independent composition, similarly incorporates the next three verses with their prefatory letters. Each reading is prefaced by 'Incipit lamentatio (*or* De lamentatione) Ieremiae prophetae' and ends with the refrain 'Ierusalem convertere ad Dominum Deum tuum'. Only in this refrain is there any trace of the plainsong intonations used for the Lamentations: elsewhere, there are minor deviations from the standard liturgical text which tend to confirm that these two settings are independent motets for use in Holy Week, rather than part of any ritual office. It is possible to go further and to maintain that they were not conceived as church music at all, but rather for private recreational singing by loyal Catholics. Several writers have expressed the rather romantic notion that the words must have sounded to Tallis 'like an almost literal description of the ruin which had befallen the ancient Church'.[7] It is true that they are perfectly capable of this symbolic

---

[6] Byrd's early *Emendemus in melius* is a third such respond, which Kerman describes as 'his only motet in the 1575 collection which gives a really strong personal impression'.

[7] H. B. Collins, 'Thomas Tallis', *Music and Letters*, x (1929), p. 163.

meaning, but doubtful whether Tallis set them with any such con-sciously emotive purpose. Polyphonic Lamentations had been widely composed in Europe since the fifteenth century: at least sixty conti-nental composers are known to have used this text, and one cannot claim any more than that Tallis, like them, was attracted to it merely because it offered excellent scope for highly expressive writing.

The psalm-motet was a similar continental genre of which English composers became aware in the mid-century years, and which this early Elizabethan generation cultivated with some enthusiasm. Although the word 'motet' was not used before Elizabeth's reign, independent set-tings of complete Latin psalms, or of sections of Psalm 118 (Vulgate numbering), had appeared under Mary and possibly even under Henry VIII. Some of the earliest, such as White's *Exaudiat te* and *Domine non est exaltatum*,[8] have many of the characteristics of the earlier votive antiphon, including the division into triple and duple halves, and the sectional treatment for full choir and solo groups (including gimel), suggesting that the psalm directly adopted both the form and function of the antiphon when the pre-Reformation Marian texts were suppres-sed. Joseph Kerman, in an important article,[9] gives reasons for thinking that it became particularly popular in the 1560s. For example, settings of nine sections of Psalm 118 may date from 1568, including four by White—now writing in a much more modern style, with no sectional treatment, but instead a continuous texture with regular imitation and skilful antiphonal effects. Two psalms by Tallis, *Domine quis habitabit* (246) and *Laudate Dominum* (266), exhibit exactly the same character-istics and almost certainly date from the same decade. *Laudate Dominum* is one of the very few such settings which include the doxology.

Although the psalm-motets were fairly clearly not designed for use as part of the daily services, they probably received fairly frequent performance in Elizabeth's chapels. There are other motets by Tallis, however, which may well have been written for special occasions. Jeremy Noble has pointed out that *Suscipe quaeso* (222) is for seven voices in almost exactly the same disposition and compass as the Mass of (probably) 1554, suggesting that it might have been designed for the same ceremonies. Its text, in the form of a collect, would have served admirably for Pole's formal absolution of the country: 'Suscipe quaeso Domine vocem confitentis; scelera mea non defendo; peccavi, peccavi, Deus miserere mei; dele culpas meas gratia tua.' The piece is in two

[8] *TCM*, v, pp. 112, 75.
[9] 'The Elizabethan motet: a study of texts for music', *Studies in the Renaissance*, ix (1962), p. 273.

distinct parts, in the manner of a continental motet, and also has a long sustained imitative opening of a kind found twice in the Mass; but other stylistic evidence is less certain. The matter remains largely speculative, for there are two textually similar 'confessional' motets, *Mihi autem nimis* (204) and *Absterge Domine* (180), which cannot on any musical grounds be assigned to Mary's reign.

The motet *Spem in alium* (299) is more obviously an occasional piece, for which various state occasions have been suggested. The extraordinary number of forty[10] voices must surely have some greater significance, however, and an attractive theory is that it was written for the fortieth birthday of a sovereign: either Mary's in 1556 or Elizabeth's in 1573. The latter is perhaps more likely, on stylistic and other grounds; and some such tribute could well have been connected with the decision of Tallis and Byrd to petition the queen, at about the same time, for a source of income in the form of a licence to print and publish music. But whatever its immediate motives, the work must surely also contain some element of personal fulfilment, satisfying that desire of so many composers in their old age to write a 'masterwork' embodying the very finest of their art.

The seven-part *Miserere nostri* (207) is another special case. Pieces called *Miserere* in sixteenth-century England, particularly those written for instruments, often incorporate the melody of the psalm-antiphon *Miserere mihi* as a cantus firmus, or employ some similar artifice just for the technical satisfaction achieved. Byrd contributed to the 1575 *Cantiones* a six-part setting of the antiphon, using both a cantus firmus and canonic treatment.[11] Tallis's, although to a different text, is obviously closely related to this category, for it is one of his very few 'demonstrations' of technical skill: a canon six-in-two, with a free tenor. The two superius voices sing a normal canon, and the discantus has a part which is also sung by three other voices starting simultaneously—one in double augmentation, one inverted and augmented, and another inverted and in triple augmentation. Again one thinks of a long continental tradition, of textures like the opening of Pierre de la Rue's *L'homme armé* Mass,[12] and sees the English, deprived of their ritual field, turning to continental forms and techniques to find a creative outlet, and taking enough pride in their skills to want to make them known, both at home and abroad.

10 The Chapel Royal had forty 'Gentlemen' for some time, but this can have no more than symbolic relevance since the motet is not performable by men only.

11 *TCM*, ix, p. 129.

12 Quoted in *Historical Anthology of Music*, i, No. 92.

Such advertisement was undoubtedly a secondary motive underlying the publication of the *Cantiones Sacrae* in 1575, even if the primary one was commercial. It was evidently a failure financially, the edition being either too small or too early to help stimulate home demand for music of high quality for recreational use. Their printer, Thomas Vautrollier, who was mainly interested in disseminating Protestant propaganda, may well have driven a hard bargain. Indeed Joseph Kerman has plausibly inferred[13] that the terms of his contract with Tallis and Byrd may even have enabled him to prevent further printing under the licence. His death in 1587 could therefore account for the sudden spate of publications from 1588 onwards; in which case it is tragic that Tallis's last years should have been clouded by such frustration.

The most fundamental stylistic development of this period was the adoption not only of the forms but also of the all-purpose, continuously-imitative texture of the continental motet. The technical challenge of a cantus firmus persisted in a limited way in Elizabethan vocal music, but became increasingly transferred to the instrumental field.

Tallis's earlier imitative style, as has been shown, parallels that of Gombert's generation in its 'purely musical' design. The words may influence the setting in very general mood or in minor details, but they in no way control it. The textual underlay is sometimes arbitrary, and the aim is an even rhythmic flow, the effect is one of tranquillity and balance. His Elizabethan music, on the other hand, is more 'modern' in the sense that the natural rhythm of the words more obviously dictates that of the music: the listener feels that they now have meaning for the composer, and that he has allowed them to suggest sharper contrasts of musical material, pace and texture. But it must be remembered that in the 1560s even the younger generation of continental composers were only just becoming aware of the range of mood and vivid pictorialism which the mature madrigal could convey. Tallis, now about sixty, must not be put into that category. There is a persistent formality about most of his melodic material, particularly the imitative ideas. The well-known opening of *Absterge Domine* (180) (Ex. 20), for example, fits the words perfectly in rhythm and melodic shape, but does not actually enhance them in the subtly imaginative ways of which Lassus[14] and Byrd were capable. This is not to say that the music lacks imagination: only that, by later standards, it lacks 'bite'. It is fair to say that the progressive refinement referred to at the end of the previous

[13] *The Elizabethan Madrigal* (New York, 1962), p. 259.
[14] Lassus's early music was certainly known in England: see J. Kerman, 'An Elizabethan edition of Lassus', *Acta Musicologica*, xxvii (1955), p. 71.

chapter is not always compensated in other ways. Tallis does however share the taste of his younger contemporaries for points based on triadic intervals, especially fourths and fifths made bold by their rhythmic context (Exx. 21 and 22), and once with an almost Beethoven-

Ex. 21   *TCM* 216

Ex. 22   *TCM* 267

ian ring (Ex. 23). The exuberant and wide-ranging melodic lines
characteristic of the Marian music (Ex. 24), are much harder to find in

Ex. 24　　　　　　　　　　　　　　　　　　　　　　　　*TCM* 239

the Elizabethan. The style is habitually mainly syllabic, with the minim
(crotchet in transcription) as the prevalent note-value. Long melismas
are sparingly but expressively used, their effect now being carefully
calculated. Indeed certain situations seem consistently to evoke them—
not only an 'Amen' or 'Alleluya', demanding obvious brilliance, but
also phrases that Tallis treats in a characteristically 'yearning' fashion,
like 'Deus noster' (192, 221) or 'Deum tuum' (122). In the *Lamentations*,
the serene and soulful melismas that traditionally clothe the Hebrew
letters are used as a deliberate foil to the expressive declamatory writing
which predominates in the verses, where the simplest chordal writing
becomes a climactic device (e.g. 121).

There are occasional instances of a true pictorialism, ranging from
a simple melodic or rhythmic figure like the dotted rhythm and sequence
of Ex. 25, or the restless bass ostinato for 'nec invenit requiem' in the
Lamentations (113), to the more whimsical variety exemplified in the

Ex. 25　　　　　　　　　　　　　　　　　　　　　　　　*TCM* 285

opening of *Derelinquat impius viam suam* (189), where the point of imitation is not only highly errant melodically but also enters on all sorts of unexpected degrees of the scale:

Ex. 26   TCM 189

This sort of thinking, however, is very far from a normal feature. In some respects Tallis is more restrained even than his pre-Reformation contemporaries, some of whom exploit the imagery of, say, the Magnificat in surprising ways. His own five-part setting (73) does little more than add a sixth voice for 'Esurientes implevit bonis'.

Tallis's harmonic language is rich and sonorous, to us often deeply sombre. However, it is perhaps the one musical resource that he is most reluctant to use for direct expressive purpose. The phrase in the *Lamentations* quoted in Ex. 27 is a memorable one (106), but it is made

Ex. 27   TCM 106

so by the rising fourths, the melismas, the slow passing-note, the rhythmic layout—in fact everything except the basic harmony, which by any standards is undistinguished. But again a slightly Beethovenian attribute suggests itself, for in its context this phrase, simple in itself, acquires a considerable pathos by virtue of its remoteness from the original key-centre (Phrygian on E). Indeed the undercurrent of shifting tonality beneath plain triadic harmony is an astonishing feature of this work. The process starts at 'Aleph' (103) where imitation at the fifth necessitates a B flat:

Ex. 28   TCM 103

This in itself is nothing remarkable, for Josquin wrote a whole Credo (that of the Mass *De beata Virgine*) round a strict canon at this interval, thereby persistently creating B flat triads. Unlike Josquin, however, Tallis gradually allows a Dorian tonality to establish itself, thence moving to 'B flat' as a tonal centre (105). The same device is exploited even more swiftly and deliberately in *In ieiunio et fletu*, which is in the 'G minor' Dorian, but which pivots its way to new triads so freely that chords as remote from each other as A flat and E major occur within a page or so (198–9). These two works, both for five men's voices in much the same compass, have a good deal in common.

The ability to design and control a large structure—this long-range planning of harmony and texture-contrasts—is perhaps Tallis's chief merit, a reward of his early training in the rather extravagant musical edifices of late-Gothic England. He is sometimes criticized for too-frequent cadential full-stops, in pieces like *Absterge Domine* (180); but this is a normal characteristic in setting any supplicatory text, and is in many ways an advanced stylistic feature. That he was equally capable of the most skilful dovetailing is shown in the first setting of *Salvator mundi* (216): indeed the only real break in this piece is before the final section, which is one of those marvellously sustained, almost Purcellian, passages that constantly sidestep an expected cadence (Ex. 29). Not surprisingly the motet was placed first in the *Cantiones Sacrae*.[15]

Both structurally and technically, *Spem in alium* is unquestionably the most stunning achievement of all. Tallis's handling of the eight five-part choirs in massive imitative expositions, spatial antiphony, and

Ex. 29 TCM 218

[15] For a detailed analysis of the fugal techniques used in this motet, see J. Kerman, 'Byrd, Tallis, and the art of imitation', *Aspects of Medieval and Renaissance Music: a Birthday Offering to Gustave Reese* (London, 1967), p. 519.

dramatic tutti entries on unexpected chords, is for once without known precedent anywhere in Europe.[16]

A word of caution might be appended to this chapter about the familiar dissonance found in Elizabethan music where a sharpened rising leading-note clashes with an unsharpened falling seventh—See Ex. 30 and also Exx. 6 and 35:

Ex. 30   TCM 210

There is no real evidence that this idiom was seriously cultivated by pre-Reformation church composers, although later scribes, by attempting to modernize the music of Fayrfax, Taverner, and others, often give the impression that it was. Between 1550 and 1575, when the powerful influence of plainsong was replaced by that of modern continental styles, it was undoubtedly a rapidly growing practice. By the end of the century Morley was loftily describing it as hackneyed.[17] A

16 For an analysis, with an illuminating diagram, see W. Gillies Whittaker, *Collected Essays* (London, 1940), p. 86. The sources of this work are discussed by B. Schofield in *The Musical Quarterly*, xxxvii (1951), p. 176. See further my article 'Tallis's "Spem in alium" and the Elizabethan Respond-Motet', *Music and Letters*, li (1970), p. 1.

17 *A Plain and Easy Introduction to Practical Music* (ed. R. A. Harman, London, 1952), p. 259.

composer like Tallis presents a serious problem, for there is some evidence that he did not expect a singer automatically to sharpen a cadential leading-note (e.g. III, bar 2, where the effect is grotesque); yet some such clashes were printed in the *Cantiones Sacrae*, presumably with his sanction. But the biting dissonance is never used to point the text: all that can be said is that it does intensify the emotional 'release' of a cadence. In any case, sources of all kinds are so capricious in their application of accidentals that it is impossible to know what Tallis's real views were. It is therefore safest to sing only such accidentals as are found in a good contemporary source like the *Cantiones Sacrae;* and those who dislike the 'depressive' effect of flat leading-notes, or who find fascination in the clashes, should reflect that such subjective arguments have no relevance whatever.

However, no textual uncertainty of this kind can in any way obscure the richness of Tallis's Latin music. We have seen the Gothic luxuriance of the antiphons, the Renaissance splendour of the 1554 Mass, the pure cold craftsmanship of the big Marian responds, the vigour and variety of a psalm like *Laudate Dominum*, the streamlined Flemish technique of the first *Salvator Mundi*, the canonic intricacy of *Miserere nostri*—the sheer versatility alone is astounding. From what scant evidence we have, Tallis was a humble, pious, and conscientious man, admired and respected by monarch, colleagues, and pupils alike. It is perhaps in some of the less obviously brilliant music of his later years—the *Lamentations*, and one or two of the hymns—that one finds the clearest reflection of his character, the art which conceals art, and the true poetry of the age.

IV

ENGLISH CHURCH MUSIC

IF Henry VIII was able to carry out fairly easily his constitutional reform of the English church, he was much slower to respond to pressures for a reformed liturgy.[1] The idea of vernacular services he associated with Lutheranism, which in turn meant radical and heretical ideas. Until the end of his reign, in fact, the English language was officially sanctioned only in the biblical lessons, the Litany,[2] and the

[1] For the most lucid account, see Owen Chadwick, *The Reformation* (*Pelican History of the Church*, iii); for a detailed one, H. Maynard Smith, *Henry VIII and the Reformation* (London, 1964).

[2] Cranmer's of 1544 seems to have been set in five parts at that time. See *NOHM*, iv, p. 498.

Primers. Even Cranmer's letter to Henry VIII of 1544, embodying his famous 'one syllable one note' principle, was concerned only with the Litany and a projected Processional.

In the reign of Edward VI (1547–53), however, a wholly vernacular liturgy was adopted. The first prayer-book was published in 1549, but replaced in 1552 by a second,[3] which contained some revised phraseology and other changes, and which later (in 1559) became the basis of the Elizabethan prayer-book. In the services proper, the main scope for polyphony lay in the five items of the Ordinary of Communion (translated from the Latin Mass) and the five canticles of Morning and Evening Prayer, all of which could be set either individually or in a musical cycle called a 'Service'. The daily psalms could also be sung in simple polyphony, as could the Responses and a few other items. The English habit of singing a votive antiphon after certain Offices also led to provision for an anthem (the same word) at the end of the new Morning and Evening Prayer.

In the composition of such polyphony the composers of the Chapel Royal were clearly prominent—notably the two older men, Tallis and Tye, but also a few younger ones such as Sheppard and Causton. They adopted a surprisingly wide range of style and method, including what may be called a 'normal' short-anthem style for four voices; some richer textures perhaps intended only for the Chapel Royal itself; and a very simple, mainly chordal style associated with psalms and certain relatively functional texts such as the Litany. Nevertheless, both anthems and cyclic Services exist in all three styles—this diversity being to a large extent a continuation of pre-Reformation practice, in which both elaborate and very modest Masses and motets served alongside humble forms such as faburden psalms. Moreover the diversity continued until well after Tallis's death, from which it follows that the texture and scale of his music can offer no guide whatever to its date. The fact that much of it is Edwardian is clear from other evidence, such as the survival of some pieces in the Wanley[4] and Lumley[5] part-books of c. 1548, or the use of text which was superseded in 1552, or by analogy with music of Sheppard, who must have died within a few months of Elizabeth's accession.

What I have called the short-anthem style is represented in seven works by Tallis.[6] Three are certainly Edwardian, viz. the anthems

---

[3] Both Edwardian prayer-books are reprinted in Everyman's Library (Dent), No. 448.

[4] Oxford, Bodleian Library Mss. Mus.Sch.420–22.

[5] Mss. Roy.App.74–6.

[6] The anthems are published in *EECM 12*, the Benedictus and other service music in *EECM 13*. References are to the second (revised) impression of 1974.

Hear the voice and prayer and *If ye love me* in the Wanley books, and also the Benedictus in the Lumley books. Four other anthems, *A new Commandment, O Lord, give thy Holy Spirit*,[7] *Purge me, O Lord*, and *Verily, verily, I say unto you* survive only in later sources and could theoretically be Elizabethan. It is, however, difficult to discern any real stylistic distinctions, except that the first group are all composed within a compass of sixteen notes (probably for broken voices) whereas three of the latter use a wider compass. The six anthems average no more than 30 bars' length in a modern edition, and all except *Verily, verily* are cast in the typical ABB pattern, in which the repeat of the 'B' section adds some substance to an otherwise slender musical form. Some chordal writing is used, often for the opening phrase; but most of the texture is evolved from rather formal imitative ideas, whose careful enunciation and cadence-patterns are reminiscent of those of certain French chansons. The Benedictus is, of course, through-composed and much longer than the anthems, and therefore illustrates best the surprising variety of musical ideas which a resourceful composer could devise within such narrow constraints. (Its opening is shown at Ex. 31.) Melisma is kept to a minimum, and normally used only for technical reasons (e.g. to produce a simultaneous cadence), not for any expressive

Ex. 31

7 Text published in *Lidley's Prayers*, 1566, but possibly in use earlier.

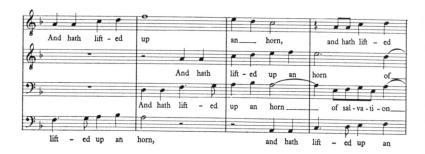

purpose. Where an imitative phrase does demand musical expansion, this is mostly achieved by text repetition rather than by melismatic extension. Both these points are illustrated in Ex. 32, from *O Lord, give thy Holy Spirit*. The harmonic language, as in much of the Latin polyphony, is almost always entirely 'neutral': only rarely is there a calculated harmonic effect like that in Ex. 33 from the Benedictus.

Ex. 32

Of the more elaborate music apparently written for the royal chapels, very little by Tallis is known. Two entire five-part Services have been lost except for the bass voice: one was entitled 'of five parts, two in one', implying that two voices were in canon throughout.[8] There is, however, a separate five-part Te Deum[9] of which enough survives to

Ex. 33

permit editorial completion, and which was probably composed before 1552, since it uses text found in the first but not the second prayer-book (such as 'Heaven and earth are *replenished with* the majesty of thy glory'). It thus belongs with a group of works, including cyclic Services by Sheppard and Robert Parsons, which illustrate the use in Edward's reign of *decani-cantoris* division of a choir. The technique involves not only block-antiphony, but also the division of the corresponding voices of each side of the choir, thus permitting very flexible vocal scoring and sometimes increasing the number of real parts to as many as seven or eight.[10] Despite its rhythmic vigour and mainly syllabic style, Tallis's Te Deum also has an expressive quality—particularly in its last four verses—which strongly foreshadows the later Lamentations.

Some half-dozen of Tallis's best-known Latin motets exist in English adaptations, details of which will be found in the List of Works.

[8] The surviving bass voice of this Service is printed in *EECM 13*, p. 179. The other (unpublished) is at Salop County Record Office, Ludlow Deposit, MS. Mus. 1: see Alan Smith, 'Elizabethan Music at Ludlow', *Music and Letters*, xlix (1969), p. 108

[9] *EECM 13*, p. 78

[10] See particularly ibid., pp. 88–90 and 101. The Magnificat and Nunc dimittis of Sheppard's Service are printed in *An Anthology of English Church Music* (ed. D. Wulstan), London, 1971, p. 59. The Nunc dimittis of Parsons's Service is in *TECM*, ii, p. 33.

Most are of pre-Restoration origin, and a few date from his lifetime and could even be his own work, for some ingenious musical emendation is occasionally found in them.[11] In the case of two other five-part works it is not clear whether an English or Latin version came first. *Blessed are they* exists only with the first six verses of the English Psalm 119, but various features of the music point to an adapted Latin form. Its smoothly-rounded entries, sustained lines, and structural antiphony between groups of three voices all have close parallels in a work like Tye's *Euge bone* Mass, and suggest an essay in continental techniques undertaken in Mary Tudor's reign (see Ex. 34). However, the reverse

Ex. 34

may be true of *I call and cry to thee, O Lord*, which was published in the 1575 *Cantiones Sacrae* with the Latin text *O sacrum convivium*. Here the English has usually been taken to be an adaptation from the Latin; but the opening point (Ex. 35a) and many details of word-setting (e.g. the bass at bar 22, Ex. 35b) make it more likely that the English version is the original one. The music is also structurally very similar to an anthem like *A new commandment*, with an ABB form, a dovetailed repeat of the 'B' section, and a brief 'coda'. If these inferences are

[11] For a good example see *TECM*, ii, p. 14, where the first *Salvator mundi* setting is printed with the variants of the English *With all our hearts and mouths*.

correct, *I call and cry* is thus the only true anthem by Tallis in more than four parts.[12]

The remainder of his Anglican music is predominantly chordal, either to create a deliberately austere or penitential mood, or to serve a functional purpose. The former category includes the 'Dorian'

Ex. 35(a)

Service, the date of which is unknown.[13] It is heavily incantatory throughout, and uses imitation only in a very limited way in its longer movements. Similar to it is the anthem (or prayer) *Remember not, O Lord God*, whose earliest version in the Lumley books is so ascetic that Day, Mulliner, and other later editors expanded it by repeating or elaborating some of its terse invocations.[14] Both these works are characterized by melodic phrases encompassing a fourth, in which respect they may well betray some influence of much-used syllabic plainsongs such as those of the Credo and Te Deum. The more functional chordal music includes two settings of the Preces and Responses, which likewise have a long history of later adaptation: both follow the normal practice of treating Marbeck's simple formulae as the tenor of the harmonization. Another such piece is the Litany, whose traditional tones originated not in Marbeck but in Cranmer's 1544 version. They are found in the tenor of most other settings, but Tallis places them in the highest of the five voices. Some sources contain four-part versions of the same music—almost certainly adaptations. The Litany was not often sung in procession at this time; moreover, it finished with the Lord's Prayer, and any setting of the so-called 'later suffrages' is not by Tallis but an editorial accretion.

[12] A bold setting of *Christ rising again*, published in *EECM 13*, p. 63, is more likely to be by Byrd.

[13] There is no source earlier than *c.* 1620 (the 'Chirk' partbooks) and textual evidence is inconclusive.

[14] *EECM 12*, p. 111 (early version) and p. 43 (Day's version); also *MB* i, p. 36 (Mulliner's keyboard reduction).

The prayer-book rubric for the daily psalms ('Then shall follow certain Psalms in order, as they be appointed . . .') was probably purposely phrased so as to allow both prose and metrical forms, sung either in unison or in simple polyphony. The many Elizabethan references to plainsong psalm-singing indicate a continuing use of the old pre-Reformation psalm-tones, just as adaptable to English prose as they had been to the Latin. Occasionally—perhaps only for major feasts—they were harmonized in measured polyphony, much as in earlier faburden techniques. Tallis himself composed a sequence of ten such festal psalms, consisting of two of those proper to Christmas Day and the four each for 24th and 26th evenings, of which only three survive complete.[15] Ex. 36 illustrates the first verse of one, set to the seventh

Ex. 36

tone in the tenor. This same music was rhythmically adapted for succeeding verses by the composer himself[16]—the plainsong tone, however, adhering to the same melodic formula throughout, without the variable inflections of the Latin. These psalms, like the Litany, have the great merit that the texture is seldom merely chordal: each voice has a sense of purpose, and a rhythmic and melodic cogency of its own.

[15] In Barnard's *First Book of Select Church Music*, 1641. One of these, *Wherewithal shall a young man*, is printed in *TECM*, ii, p. 8. All three are in *EECM 13*, pp. 125-43. Of the other seven only the bass voice is known, the first verse of each being given in *EECM 13*, p. 189 (Nos. 16-22).

[16] The method is clearly an important antecedent of Anglican chanting, which developed in the seventeenth century.

To judge from the flood of Elizabethan prints, metrical psalms were just as popular as the biblical prose. Those of Sternhold and Hopkins were published in 1562, with a simple melody for each. A year later Day issued his *Whole Psalms in Four Parts* in which these same melodies were harmonized. Most of the harmonizations were the work of William Parsons; but one, *O Lord in thee is all my trust*, is attributed to Tallis.[17] In 1567 another metrical psalter, that of Archbishop Parker, was supplied by Tallis with eight four-part tunes, in various modes, moods and metres (all specified), and a ninth—now known as the 'Ordinal'—for *Come Holy Ghost*. Most are in current use as hymn-tunes, the *English Hymnal* alone containing six (Hymns 3, 46, 78, 92, 267, and 496). A note in the psalter points out that the tenor of each is the principal melody, and in some modern versions the treble and tenor are interchanged, including the eighth, in which these two voices constitute the famous canon. The third tune, made even more famous by Vaughan Williams, is used in both forms. Modern usage has also shortened some by omitting repeated phrases; but despite the vicissitudes of time they remain among the very best of early harmonized tunes for congregational use, a perfect demonstration of the art of simplicity.[18]

Closely related to the English church music are four secular part-songs which survive as keyboard reductions in *The Mulliner Book*,[19] a manuscript anthology compiled by the Elizabethan organist Thomas Mulliner. Of these, only *When shall my sorrowful sighing* can be found with its text in contemporary vocal sources (the earliest being the Lumley books, to which it is however a late addition). The origin of the verse is unknown, but the use of imitation and expressive melisma gives the music clear affinities with the Elizabethan consort songs. *Like as the doleful dove* is a virtually chordal setting of some colourfully penitential verse by William Hunnis, a Chapel Royal colleague. *O ye tender babes* is an oddity: a prose text beginning with these words has been found (in, somewhat improbably, a grammar book published in 1542/3), but it does not fit comfortably with Mulliner's version of the music.[20] The last, *Fond youth is a bubble*, is a secular adaptation of the anthem *Purge me, O Lord*.

[17] *EECM 12*, p. 29.

[18] A facsimile of the first tune is in *MGG* ('Tallis'). All nine are transcribed and discussed by Ellinwood in 'Tallis's Tunes and Tudor Psalmody', *Music Disciplina*, ii (1948), p. 189; and printed in *EECM 13*, p. 160.

[19] Published as *MB* i. The four pieces mentioned are on pp. 63, 84, 61 and 21 respectively. They are printed in vocal form in *EECM 12*, pp. 95–110.

[20] See Denis Stevens, 'A musical admonition for Tudor schoolboys', *Music and Letters*, xxxvii (1957), p. 49.

These secular partsongs aptly portray what C. S. Lewis called the 'drab age'. The vigour and raciness of those of Cornysh's generation has been suppressed by a sternly moral tone; nor is there yet much trace of the metrical control, poise, and variety of the music and verse of the madrigal era. In the creation of a new repertory for the Anglican church, however, Tallis's achievement was unequalled. He had no evident Protestant sympathies, but he accepted the new regime much as a modern civil servant accepts a change of government. The demand for the utmost clarity imposed a stringent discipline on the technique of all composers, but very few were able to transcend such ideological considerations and inject subtle artistry into even the simplest forms. John Day, and later Barnard and Boyce, placed Tallis's work first in their anthologies of English church music, tacitly accepting his primacy among the first generation of its composers.

V

INSTRUMENTAL MUSIC

THE first two chapters stressed the role of much of Tallis's earlier Latin church music as something integral to the liturgy, adorning or replacing the ritual plainsong. For half a century or more before 1559, however, it was not uncommon for monastic and some other institutions to use an organ instead of a choir for this purpose, chiefly in office hymns and antiphons. The organ polyphony normally incorporated the relevant plainsong, though occasionally a faburden-derivative was used instead. Tallis himself apparently fulfilled organ-playing duties at most stages of his earlier career, so that the surviving five antiphons and seven hymn-verses[1] probably constitute a mere fraction of his output.

We have three settings of the Lent Magnificat-antiphon *Clarifica me pater* (99, 101, 104) each with the plainsong as tenor cantus firmus surrounded by three imitative parts which develop a particular 'point' or motive right through the piece:

Ex. 37
(a) *first setting:*   MB i, 74

(b) *third setting:*   MB i, 76

[1] All except one antiphon are in the *Mulliner Book* (see Ch. IV, note 16) to which figures in brackets refer. Tallis's keyboard music has been collected into one volume by Denis Stevens in *Thomas Tallis: Complete Keyboard Works* (London, 1953). For a brief discussion see his article in *The Musical Times*, No. 1313 (July, 1952), p. 303. In addition to the part-songs, two 'sacred' pieces in Mulliner are also arrangements from vocal music, viz. no. 43 from the anthem *Remember not*, and no. 119 from *Salve intemerata* (151).

Natus est nobis (9) adds only one very florid line to the plainsong (which is laid out in trochaic metre), and *Gloria tibi trinitas* is in two semi-canonic parts which vigorously paraphrase the well-known plainsong. In this liturgical organ music Tallis shows little concern with the more idiomatic keyboard material of Redford and some other contemporaries. The hymn-verses[2] are even more consistently vocal, in a smooth imitative texture. Their plainsong is always clearly present in outline, but not without various interpolated points, extra notes, rhythmic elasticity, and other adaptation.

The Tallis pieces are noticeably concentrated towards the end of Mulliner's anthology, suggesting that he may have come across them at a late stage in his compilation of the MS. Whilst this is in itself no evidence of the date of composition, two factors—the assured handling of a continuously pointed texture, and the absence of faburdens—tend to confirm that most are relatively late, possibly even Marian. The dispersal of choirs in the 1540s may have helped to produce a strong revival of organ polyphony in her reign, and the presence of the Spanish organist Cabezon in London at that time can hardly have failed to stimulate interest.[3]

There were two quite distinct phases of Tudor keyboard music: the pre-1559 liturgical organ music represented in the *Mulliner Book*, and the rich Elizabethan repertory of secular pieces for the virginals, collected in the *Fitzwilliam Virginal Book* and elsewhere. The latter source contains Tallis's two largest and most important keyboard compositions, the settings of *Felix namque*, dated (in the MS.) 1562 and 1564 respectively. Although constructed on the plainsong of the Offertory, they are clearly virginal music for recreational playing: their enormous size and virtuoso style completely rule out liturgical use. Indeed they might even be viewed as technical studies for both composer and performer, since each explores almost every facet of keyboard texture and technique then known.

The term 'variation' is not strictly applicable, there being no repetition of any material: the long plainsong melody is set out only once in

---

[2] *Mulliner Book*, nos. 86, 97, 100, 102, 105 and 106. None is a complete composition, however. The liturgical organ book MS. Add. 29996 (*EECM*, vi, edited by John Caldwell) makes it clear that the organ always deputized for the priest's side of the choir, thus replacing the odd-numbered verses and acting as 'ruler' as well. Mulliner evidently selected verses casually for his anthology: for example, the two *Ecce tempus idoneum* verses are probably from the same organ-setting of that hymn, but three would be needed to provide a complete scheme for the five verses.

[3] Various scholars have tried to establish mutual influences, but there is not enough material for a valid comparison.

each piece. In the first setting, the incipit appears in the tenor; the next three notes (G, F, B flat) form an imitative set of entries; and thereafter the plainsong continues as an unadorned treble cantus firmus, each note of the melody becoming two minims in transcription. Against it the lower parts explore between thirty and forty different rhythmic and melodic patterns of the kind familiar in later virginal variations—some fairly chordal, some imitative, some hocketing, others just broken chords or running toccata-like flourishes and sequences. Each texture lasts for anything from three to eight notes of the plainsong, sometimes merging imperceptibly into the next by simple melodic extension, sometimes effecting a dramatic change. Formal cohesion is achieved by mensuration changes: the first third is duple, the last third triple, and the middle oscillates restlessly between the two. The second *Felix namque* is similar in principle, but here the plainsong is an inside part, freeing the right hand for even more brilliant writing. On paper and on a piano this is rambling and monotonous music, but on an instrument of the harpsichord family, played with both rhythmic panache and a feeling for beauty of detail, it is powerful and impressive. It is impossible to illustrate more than a fragment, taken from the second working (Ex. 38).

Ex. 38

There is one other very brilliant piece called a 'Lesson', which one source erroneously attributes to Bull. Even if it served a pedagogical function, this too is a study in composition, for it consists of two canonic parts for the right hand, joined after a few bars by continuous semiquavers (of transcription) in the left. The progressive rhythmic tension of the canonic parts is astonishingly well controlled.

Virginal playing already had a fairly long history in England. To judge from her account books[4] and from chroniclers' references, Mary Tudor was an accomplished performer (probably much more so than her younger half-sister) and may well have encouraged her musicians to write for the instrument. Tallis thus emerges as one of the main carriers of a tradition developing continuously from Aston to Bull, in which the *Felix namque* pieces provide a vital link. It is almost impossible to cite any contemporary continental music which matches them in either keyboard technique or fertility of invention.

There are enough *Felix namque* workings by other composers to suggest a tradition of recreational 'exercises'; but it never achieved anything like the popularity or longevity of the comparable form for viols, the *In nomine*. Cultivated in earnest from the mid-sixteenth century onwards, the *In nomine* produced a rich crop from Tallis's Chapel Royal colleagues of all ages. For Tye, in particular, it held a strong fascination. There are only two by Tallis, plus a third piece based on a different plainsong, *Libera nos, salva nos*.[5] All three are quietly imitative around a cantus firmus, with only occasional traces of a developing instrumental idiom (see Ex. 39, treble)—for the viols, by nature a polyphonic and 'vocal' medium, were much slower than the keyboard to move away from a vocal style. Nevertheless Tye and some

Ex. 39
(note-values 1/4)

Bodl. MS. Mus. d. 212-6

[4] *Privy Purse Expenses of the Princess Mary*, 1536–44, ed F. Madden (London, 1831).

[5] Found only in MSS. Add. 37402–6, and of doubtful authenticity.

younger contemporaries were beginning to use the *In nomine* as a vehicle for rhythmic complexity and florid display. Tallis's unobtrusive mastery contrasts notably with their novelty-seeking manner, and reveals a fundamentally different musical personality.

Tallis, by temperament and training, belonged to a late-medieval generation of monastic musicians to whom novelty as such was no more a virtue in music than in any other sphere of religious life. When he moved to the court, the cultural centre of the realm, there were isolated occasions when he clearly sought to impress, and which produced the seven-part Mass and *Spem in alium*. In general, however, his vocal music is characterized by a restraint, a deliberately undemonstrative quality, that has sometimes been stigmatized as dullness. He clearly kept pace with musical developments during his long life; but the very great difficulty of dating music (even within a decade or so) makes it impossible to assess how far he pioneered new ideas in England, and how far he merely absorbed and synthesized those of others. Certainly many of the technical and stylistic features pointed out in the different stages of his composition can be found more sharply defined in the work of contemporaries—successively Taverner, Sheppard, and later Parsons and Byrd. However, it was apparently not until the second half of Elizabeth's reign that composers became particularly conscious of the concept of 'pioneering'. Only in a handful of Tallis's late pieces (mainly those for the keyboard) is there any real glimpse of a new competitive spirit, a new pride in individual achievement, that was to become very strong indeed in the mature music of Byrd—as in most other fields of artistic endeavour—in the three or four decades after Tallis's death.

The names of Tallis and Byrd have been closely associated ever since the appearance of the *Cantiones Sacrae* in 1575; but they have no more in common than Haydn and Beethoven—who incidentally differed in age by an almost identical margin (thirty-eight years). Byrd and Beethoven each epitomized a new era, and both brought to music a powerful personality, a new humanist spirit, and a new intensity and range of imaginative power expressed through classical perfection of technique. Tallis and Haydn, on the other hand, shared a more detached view of their art. For more than half his career Tallis was constrained by the dictates of the most formal religious observance, Haydn by the refined taste of the Esterhazy family; and both had therefore been conditioned by a training in composition of a relatively functional kind. Yet both, in their later years, were able to transcend an established musical language by rethinking routine methods and by using new resources of composition (like modulation to remote keys) in a way which never disturbs the symmetry and poise of their music. There is in each the dedication of the mature craftsman, who made contact with—but could not accept—the bolder musical thinking of a much younger man, yet whose music is suffused by a warmth and humanity, sometimes by wit, and almost always by a deeply poetic quality that place it among the most enduring products of its age.

REFERENCES

A bibliography is not provided, most important books, articles, and editions of music being referred to in the footnotes. All manuscripts mentioned are at the British Museum unless otherwise stated. I have used the following abbreviations for reference to the printed and MS. sources indicated. Although they are seldom specifically acknowledged, I should like to express an especial debt to *MMB* and *MR*, both indispensable to anybody working in this field.

AS : Antiphonale Sarisburiensis, ed. W. H. Frere, 3 vols., London, 1901–25.
Cantiones Sacrae : T. Tallis and W. Byrd, *Cantiones quae ab argumento sacrae vocantur*, London, 1575.
Christ Church partbooks: Christ Church, Oxford, MSS. 979–83 and 984–8.
EECM : Early English Church Music, London, 1963–.
Gyffard partbooks (1553–8): British Museum MSS. Add. 17802–5.
MB : Musica Britannica, London, 1951–.
MMB : F. Ll. Harrison, *Music in Medieval Britain*, London, 2nd revised edition, 1962.
MGG : Die Musik in Geschichte und Gegenwart, 1949–68.
MR : Gustave Reese, *Music in the Renaissance*, London, 1959.
Mulliner Book : British Museum MS. Add. 30513.
NOHM : New Oxford History of Music, London. (References are to Vol. iv, 1968.)
Peterhouse partbooks (*c.* 1540): Peterhouse, Cambridge, MSS. 40, 41, 31, 32.
TCM : Tudor Church Music, 10 vols., London, 1923–9, and *Appendix*, 1948. (References are to Vol. vi unless otherwise stated.)
TECM : Treasury of English Church Music, 5 vols., London, 1965.
Wanley partbooks (1547–9): Oxford, Bodleian Library, MSS. Mus. e. 420–2.

General accounts will also be found in E. H. Fellowes, *English Cathedral Music* new edition revised by J. A. Westrup, London, 1969; Denis Stevens, *Tudor Church Music* (London, 1961); and Ernest Walker, *A History of Music in England* (3rd edition revised by J. A. Westrup, London, 1952). A particularly valuable account of the English church music of this period will be found in Peter le Huray, *Music and the Reformation in England, 1549–1660* (London, 1967).

LIST OF WORKS

(The last column provides an index to references in this volume)

Key to symbols
A   adapted to new text (with number of original)
C   included in *Cantiones Sacrae*, 1575
d   defective (e.g. one voice missing) but restorable editorially
D   more seriously defective: not restorable at present
f   fragment of larger polyphonic composition
l   larger form
s   smaller form
u   uncertain authorship, but probably Tallis

Sources
(*Note:* sources are not given except to identify keyboard pieces)
Add 31403   British Museum MS. Add. 31403
ChCh 371   Christ Church Oxford, MS. 371
F   page reference to *The Fitzwilliam Virginal Book*, 2 vols, London, 1894
M   number in *The Mulliner Book, MB* i

A. Pre-Elizabethan Latin Church Music

			Voices	Liturgical form		TCM	page
1.	*u*	Alleluia, ora pro nobis	4	(for Lady-Mass)		88	36
2.		Audivi vocem	4	respond	(*s*)	90	29f.
3.	*D*	Ave Dei patris filia	5	antiphon	(*l*)	162	12ff.
4.	*d*	Ave rosa sine spinis	5	antiphon	(*l*)	169	12ff.
5.	*C*	Candidi facti sunt	5	respond	(*l*)	186	32
6.	*du*	Deus tuorum militum	5	hymn		264	34
7.	*C*	Dum transisset sabbatum	5	respond	(*l*)	257	32
8.	*f*	Euge caeli porta	4	sequence-verse		179	36
9.		Gaude gloriosa	6	antiphon	(*l*)	123	12ff.
10.		Hodie nobis caelorum rex	4	respond	(*s*)	92	29ff.

11.		Homo quidam fecit coenam	6	respond	(*l*)	282	32
12.	C	Honor virtus et potestas	5	respond	(*l*)	237	32f.
13.		Iam Christus astra ascenderat	5	hymn		285	34ff.
14.		Iesu salvator saeculi	5	hymn		289	34
15.		In pace si dedero	4	respond	(*s*)	94	29ff.
16.		Loquebantur variis linguis	7	respond	(*l*)	272	32f.
17.		Magnificat	4	canticle	(*s*)	64	26ff.
18.		Mass	4		(*s*)	31	19f.
19.		Mass, *Puer natus est nobis*	7		(*l*)	49	20ff.
		Gloria					
	D	Credo					
	d	Sanctus					
	D	Agnus Dei					
20.	d	Mass, *Salve intemerata virgo*	5		(*l*)	3	17f.
21.		Quod chorus vatum	5	hymn		261	34
22.		Salvator mundi Domine	5	hymn		242	34f.
23.		Salve intemerata virgo	5	antiphon	(*l*)	144	12ff.
24.		Sancte Deus	4	antiphon	(*s*)	98	15
25.	C	Sermone blando angelus	5	hymn		193	34ff.
26.	C	Te lucis ante terminum I	5	hymn		214	34ff.
27.	C	Te lucis ante terminum II	5	hymn		215	34ff.
28.		Videte miraculum	6	respond	(*l*)	293	32f.

B. Elizabethan Latin Vocal Music

			Voices	Source of text	TCM	page
29.	C	Absterge Domine	5	prayer	180	41, 47
30.	C	Derelinquat impius	5	respond (Roman)	189	39, 45
31.		Domine quis habitabit	5	Psalm xiv	246	40
32.	C	In ieiunio et fletu	5	respond (Roman)	198	39, 46
33.	C	In manus tuas	5	respond	202	38
34.		Lamentations (1st set)	5	lesson (Tenebrae)	102	39, 44
35.		Lamentations (2nd set)	5	lesson (Tenebrae)	110	39, 44
36.		Laudate Dominum	5	Psalm cxvi	266	40
37.	d	Magnificat & Nunc dimittis	5	Latin prayerbook	73	38, 45
38.	C	Mihi autem nimis	5	introit	204	41
39.	C	Miserere nostri	7	prayer	207	41
40.	C	O nata lux de lumine	5	hymn	209	36
41.	C	O sacrum convivium	5	Magnificat-antiphon	210	38
42.		O salutaris hostia	5	hymn	276	38
43.	C	Salvator mundi salva nos I	5	psalm-antiphon	216	38, 47
44.	C	Salvator mundi salva nos II	5	psalm-antiphon	219	38
45.		Spem in alium	40	respond	299	41, 47
46.	C	Suscipe quaeso (two parts)	7	prayer	222	40

C. English Service Music

D. English Anthems

E. Early Adaptations of Latin Motets *(See pp. 53–4)*

F. Secular Partsongs *(See p.57)*

G. Keyboard Music

Lord, for thy tender mercy's sake	Hilton
Not every one that saith (printed *EECM 13*, p. 190)	
O God, be merciful	Tye
O Lord God of hosts	? (17th-century)
O Lord, I bow the knee	William Mundy
O sing unto the Lord	Probably Sheppard
O thou God almighty	Hooper
Out from the deep (printed *EECM 12*, p. 35)	Probably William Parsons
Submit yourselves to one another	Sheppard
The simple sheep that went astray (words only known)	
This is my commandment	Probably William Mundy